VERY BRITISH PROBLEMS

VOLUME 3

STILL AWKWARD, STILL RAINING

ROB TEMPLE

Illustrations by Andrew Wightman

sphere

SPHERE

First published in Great Britain in 2017 by Sphere

Text copyright © Rob Temple 2017
Illustrations © Andrew Wightman 2017

1 3 5 7 9 10 8 6 4 2

A CIP catalogue record for this book
is available from the British Library.

ISBN 978-0-7515-7012-0

Typeset in Caslon by M Rules
Printed and bound in Great Britain by
Clays Ltd, St Ives plc

Papers used by Sphere are from well-managed forests
and other responsible sources.

Sphere
An imprint of
Little, Brown Book Group
Carmelite House
50 Victoria Embankment
London EC4Y 0DZ

An Hachette UK Company
www.hachette.co.uk

www.littlebrown.co.uk

For Rhiain & Raffy

CONTENTS

INTRODUCTION

Welcome to *Very British Problems Volume III*, come in and make yourself at home. But first take off your shoes. And stay out of the cupboards. And ... look, just sit down.

It's been a whirlwind (or at least a stiff breeze) of activity since we started documenting VBPs all the way back in the glorious year of 2012. As the world has changed, some might say in a terrifying way, our British quirks and obsessions have only escalated. The @SoVeryBritish Twitter account, Facebook page and Instagram feed have a combined following of almost three million sufferers, locked together in an endless muddle of baffling behaviour, all more awkward than a giraffe on a penny farthing.

And here we have a whole new shiny tome of VBPs, in every situation imaginable, from January dieting to Christmas excess. Also inside you'll find the 10 Stages of British Anger, the Very British 'How To' Guide to Everything, a handy email translation guide, a detailed history of the British relationship with tea and also some boozy British cocktails to see us through.

If you've received this book as a Christmas present, that means the person who gave it to you thinks you have a serious case of the VBPs. You'll have proved their suspicions right when you opened the wrapping, tried to smile, held the book up for a bit for no real reason and then turned red because everyone was looking at you: the true VBP method of accepting a gift.

If you bought it for yourself, I hope you feel better soon.

Anyway ... never really sure how to end these things. Could just stop typing, perhaps? Not sure. Well, this is uncomfortable. Look, just go to one of the proper chapters ... thanks.

Rob Temple, Cambridge, 2017

1. EXERCISE

Attempting a slightly heavier bench press than usual and making a noise like you've just given birth to a bicycle.

Wondering why you don't seem to be losing any weight when you've committed to sitting still on an exercise bike for at least an hour every single day.

Spending the majority of any tennis match you play holding your arm aloft and shouting sorry.

Seeing your occasional 20-minute jog as an excuse to eat 12 sausages and a kilo of mash for lunch.

The embarrassment of noticing that a pile of Quality Street wrappers has fallen out of your pockets while you've been going hell for leather on the rowing machine.

Thinking that you're still fantastic at rugby because you played it for a year when you were eight.

Losing so much oxygen attempting to say good morning to other runners that you have to stop to pass out in a hedge.

The humiliation of attempting one chin-up.

Suspecting you might be doing catastrophic damage to your ligaments every time you do the stretching exercises you invented.

Forgetting to turn on your fitness tracking app and live Facebook route updates, meaning the 22 miles you just ran count for nothing.

Getting into your exercise kit and watching telly until it's time for bed.

Accepting the
inevitable fate that
now you've decided
to run two miles
a week, all your
birthday presents for
ever more will be
running socks.

**Being unable to wait until you've
fully exited the gym before
tucking into your ham rolls.**

Causing so much distress to your
fellow swimmers while attempting
to do the butterfly that you're
asked to leave the pool.

Thinking your luminous running jacket
is too jazzy, so swapping it for a black one
and taking your chances with oncoming
traffic.

Thinking you can run off a
hangover and finding yourself in a
field half a mile from your house,
unable to move.

Hoping that a bottle of Lucozade and a handful of Skittles on the day will make up for doing no marathon training whatsoever.

Wondering if the people in the fitness videos you watch online have six cheat days too.

Attempting to leave the pool without using the steps and beaching yourself on the side like a sad whale.

Using your exercise bike solely for hanging washing on.

Having a ten-minute kickabout and rendering yourself unable to walk for the next four days.

2. WEATHER

Types of British weather:
Boiling out there
Sunny earlier
Colder than it looks
Chucking it down
So grey
Quite mild
Bit chilly
Bloody freezing

Removing a pair of shorts from your wardrobe and instantly triggering 40 days of biblical storms.

Yearly weather forecast: Grey with outbreaks of grey, turning more grey as the day goes on with dark grey to look forward to later.

'Ooh, you've caught the sun!'
Translation: The heat coming from your face could toast a sandwich.

Journeying to the window every now and then to give the weather a damn good frowning.

Rushing home from work in the summer to sit outside and bask in the glorious cold dusk.

Shielding yourself from a ferocious downpour by hunching your shoulders and squinting.

Describing the weather as 'a bit blustery' as your eyebrows get blown into space.

'Miserable out there, isn't it?'

'Yeah.'

(Both Brits stare out of the window for five seconds, then return silently to work.)

Making sure to say 'Bit wet out there' to everyone you see when you come in absolutely drenched.

Becoming so hot during a heatwave that you briefly consider rolling up your sleeves.

Describing hail of any circumference as 'the size of golf balls'.

Burning 50,000 calories during a hot night transferring your legs in and out of the duvet.

Feeling the need to film heavy rain on your phone's video recorder.

Being informed by the news that Britain is currently hotter than other places in the world that at other times of the year get very hot.

Reporting to everyone you know that you 'Saw a guy in shorts earlier!' on a slightly chilly day.

Stepping on a slightly loose paving slab and unleashing the North Sea.

Informing everyone you've ever met that you had to put the heating on last night.

Treating your car's thermostat as the holy grail of accurate temperature measuring devices.

'I think it might rain later.'
Translation: I live in Britain.

3. BRITAIN IN NUMBERS

The data that makes Brits British . . .

Surprise: Brits drink a lot of tea
60.2 billion cups a year
165 million cups a day

UK Tea & Infusions Association

But do Brits actually like tea?
Tea is everything! – 35%
Yes, it's lovely – 35%
Take it or leave it – 14%
Ghastly stuff – 16%

@SoVeryBritish poll, 2017: 40,276 votes

70% of Brits are unable to believe how dark it is

November 2016: 12,076 votes

Milk in first!
… So say 84% of Brits

@SoVeryBritish poll, 2015: 41,263 votes

2800 MW
Largest recorded electric kettle surge
England v West Germany, FIFA World
Cup semi-final penalty shoot-out, 4 July
1990

99
Percentage of UK households that bought
biscuits in 2016

@SoVeryBritish poll

124 cm
Width of the largest ever Jaffa Cake,
made by former *Great British Bake Off*
winner Frances Quinn in 2017

Guinness World Records

Winner, winner, beef dinner
Britain's favourite Sunday roast meat:
Beef – 39%
Chicken – 33%
Lamb – 19%
Pork – 9%

@SoVeryBritish poll, 2016: 36,612 votes

£17,181
The amount of money the average Brit
will spend on haircuts in their lifetime

Quidco survey, 2016

0
The amount of haircuts the average Brit
will be happy with

> Personal experience

> **18 hours per year**
> Amount of time the average Brit stands in
> a queue

> Study by Visa, 2014

'Sorry about the mess'
57% of Brits avoid having friends over due
to the state of their house

Vodafone survey, 2016

74.5 miles
There is nowhere in Britain that is more
than this distance to the sea

Most accurate maps

Sliced white bread!
According to you, bacon sandwiches
should be made with sliced white
bread (46%), roll (31%), toast (20%), or
something else entirely (3%)

@SoVeryBritish poll, 2016: 46,448 votes

Four months
How long Brits spend during their lives
complaining about the weather

Wilkinson survey, 2013

**The sauce that belongs on a bacon
sandwich:**
Red – 61%
Brown – 39%

@SoVeryBritish poll, 2015: 38,739 votes

Summer loving!
Best season?
Summer – 41%
Spring – 23%
Autumn – 23%
Winter – 13%

@SoVeryBritish poll, 2016: 45,759 votes

38.5°C/101.3°F
Hottest day on record
Faversham, Kent, 10 August 2003

–27.2°C/–17.0°F
Coldest days on record
Braemar, Aberdeenshire, 1895/1982
Altnaharra, Sutherland, 1995

80,000
Umbrellas lost annually on the tube

University of Westminster

Over half of Brits (51%) think cheese and beans is the best jacket potato topping

@SoVeryBritish poll, 2016: 41,044 votes

Pineapple on pizza
53% of Brits say 'yes please'

YouGov poll, 2017

156.2 days per year
Average amount it rains in Britain

Met Office

Lifetime trips to the pub: 3,386
Hangovers: 1,793

Quidco survey, 2016

4. COMMUTING

Frantically looking in every single pocket before realising your train ticket is in your mouth.

Having to venture so deep into the railway station car park that you end up back home.

Reacting as if you've just pulled the pin on a grenade when accidentally disconnecting your headphones on a quiet train.

Feeling like you're walking on stage upon entering a packed bus.

Read platform number.
Hear platform number.
Walk to that platform.
Reread platform number.
Get on train at platform.
Worry you're on wrong train.

Bumping into a colleague on the platform,
meaning your 30-minute train journey
will now seem to last about four years.

Burning around 300 calories
tensing your leg in order to stop it
touching your fellow passenger.

Wondering what contains more bacteria:
a hospital bin, a festival toilet or a fold-
down tray table.

Trying to be so casual about hailing the bus that it looks as if you're signalling to an auctioneer.

Travelling on a tube so packed you're forced to stand with your nose nestled in a stranger's ear.

Trains delayed due to:
Wrong kind of sun
Ominous cloud
Slightly damp leaf
Chilly track
Suspicious gravel
Sarcastic swan

**Feeling the need to mumble
your train's platform number to
yourself the second it appears on
the board.**

Being the world's leading expert on what other drivers could fit a bus through.

Wanting to cycle to work in a city but noticing that everyone else who does so seems to be Tour de France standard.

Having the same confidence in the tray table as you would if your coffee was balanced on the back of your hand.

'Sorry I'm late, traffic was terrible.'
Translation: I hit 'snooze' a record 23 times.

Things most frequently said while driving to and from work:
'Oh, come on, mate.'
'What is he doing?'
'Don't indicate then.'
'Idiot.'
'After you then.'

Trying to resist the regular nightly urge to secretly eat a whole Upper Crust baguette, despite only being 25 minutes away from dinner.

The only two descriptions of traffic:
1. 'Wasn't too bad actually.'
2. 'Absolute nightmare.'

Nearly having a panic attack when you hear 'Tickets, please!' as you sit in the correct seat holding your fully valid ticket.

Worrying if the smell of your burger and chips somehow breaks the rules of the quiet carriage.

5. AT THE CINEMA

Thinking you've picked a good seat until someone the size of the Statue of Liberty sits in front of you.

Deciding to get a small popcorn and a drink then remembering you don't have £84 in your wallet.

Being unable to enter the cinema without immediately worrying that you've left something on that could burn down your house.

Consuming a colourful ice drink, meaning you suddenly contain more sugar than the Stay Puft Marshmallow Man.

Saying 'I think these are our seats' about the seats that feature the exact letters and numbers as the ones on your tickets.

Wondering if the day will ever come when you manage to watch a whole film without kicking over your drink.

Finding someone in your seat and going home immediately to pre-order the DVD.

Feeling like you're smuggling cocaine across the border as you sneak in half a packet of shop-bought wine gums.

Dealing with someone kicking the back of your seat by silently clenching your teeth to dust.

Feeling the need to say 'That's coming out soon' after watching a trailer about a film that's advertised as coming out soon.

Looking in the cinema toilet mirror after the screening and noticing you seem to have the complexion of a deceased person.

Thinking there should be some kind of register for the handful of people who have ever ordered a cinema hot dog.

Getting to the car park after watching an action film and having a strong urge to roll over your bonnet and kick someone in the face.

Being unable to go to the cinema without trying to recall the date of the last time you went to the cinema.

Completely missing the film as you vividly imagine scenarios in which you give the noisy popcorn rustler a good telling-off.

Feeling the need to duck down slightly as you exit to use the loo, despite the screen being larger than your house.

'Okay, you need to go to Screen
Six. Enjoy the film.'
'Thanks, you too!'

Unexpectedly crunching on an unpopped
bit of corn and trying not to react, despite
feeling like you've fractured your jaw.

Waiting until you're halfway to the car before giving a review of 'Well, that was rubbish.'

Wondering if you can sell the 50 quid's worth of popcorn that's stuck to your jumper back to the cinema.

6. DISCUSSING POLITICS

Starting a political conversation with 'The way I look at it ...' to indicate you're about to ruin the dinner party.

Reading the voting slip 34 times before putting a cross in the wrong bit.

Thinking *Question Time* would be more honest if the panellists just said 'We don't have a clue what's going on' for 60 minutes.

Wondering who'll be the next US president: Darth Vader, a machine gun with a face, or an angry shark.

Exiting a political chat in which you've become quickly out of your depth by saying 'Well, they're all as bad as each other.'

Seeing an article titled 'What the budget means for you' and having a hunch it probably won't mean more money.

Regretting staying up all night to watch election results when you hear 'It could go either way' for the hundredth time at 5 a.m.

Searching the house from top to bottom before discovering you've been using your polling card as a coaster for the past three months.

Hearing the words 'Brexit' and 'referendum' more times in the past few years than you've heard your own name.

Knowing you've been listening to politicians far too much lately when you start prefixing everything you say with 'look'.

Listening to a colleague's political opinions and using all your might to stop yourself going full Paxman.

Pausing before depositing your voting slip at the polling booth, just to be 100 per cent sure you're not actually posting your house keys into a postbox.

Wondering why you never see the residents of Downing Street putting out their bins.

Looking back with fondness at
the innocent days when the messy
consumption of a bacon sandwich was
headline news.

Accidentally sharing a political
opinion on social media and taking
the decision to bury your phone
after three days of notifications.

Wondering what would help you predict an election outcome more accurately: looking at the polls, or observing some tea leaves that you've thrown in the sink.

Feeling your brain starting to melt like grilled cheese while someone explains how US voting works.

'It didn't quite go as planned.'
Translation: We may have caused irreversible damage on a monumental scale.

Being unable to put your voting
slip into what is quite clearly the
ballot box without saying 'Do I just
pop this in here?'

7. THE 10 STAGES OF BRITISH ANGER

If you meet a Brit who's anywhere above stage 4, run away . . .

Stage 1: Slightly put out

This is where the anger begins, and it can and will spiral quickly from here. Perhaps a neighbour has parked his car in the Brit's usual spot. Maybe a colleague has taken a favourite pen. There is a suspicion that someone isn't pulling their weight when it comes to the tea run. It will only be a relatively minor incident, but it will sow a seed; once slightly put out, a Brit will not rest until vengeance is served. Often when slightly put out, a Brit will tut, and that's when you'll know that all hell is about to break loose.

Stage 2: Miffed

You can't stay slightly put out for ever; the state of miffed will quickly follow as the rage has been allowed to ferment. If, say, the situations listed in stage 1 weren't just one-off incidents but have somehow happened again, then a Brit's blood starts to boil and their body starts to tremble, much like a kettle. At this stage, the Brit will start to think about saying something, before trying to quash that idea completely. Eyes will slightly narrow, a plan will be formed and arms may very well become folded.

Stage 3: Disgruntled

This is the stage where the rising anger will start to become verbalised. The Brit will mutter, almost inaudibly, short phrases such as 'I don't know', 'Oh, come on' and 'That's not on'. When a Brit is disgruntled, he/she will want other people to know and, ideally, join in the disgruntlement. Situations that classically lead to this stage include the announcement of the cancellation of an oft-cancelled train, or the arrival of a 'sorry we missed you' delivery note when the Brit has been at home, by the door, all day.

Stage 4: Cross

Careful now, things are getting real. Once at the cross stage, the anger is rarely able to be reversed quickly. Once cross, a Brit will turn red, become sweaty and start to utter mild swear words. Look very closely and you may even notice a twitching eye or a shaking fist. This is also the stage where a Brit will start to formulate a plan of complaint, seeking out the best person to have a bit of a shout at. He/she will shake their head, roll their eyes and, for some reason, look at their watch a lot. They will also text a loved one and somehow blame the situation on them.

Stage 5: Exasperated

At this stage, a Brit might crouch down, put head in hands or even laugh incredulously at the situation. They'll start bargaining with nobody, and declare the situation 'bloody typical, just sodding bloody typical', even if it's the first time it's ever happened. The head shake will now be constant and arms will be sporadically thrown skywards. The Brit may even hold their arms in the air and spin around, as if doing some kind of angry goal celebration, as a warning to those nearby to leave them alone.

Stage 6: Fuming

The Brit is now a pressure cooker stuffed full of incandescent fury. Only approach if you have a solution to the problem. The Brit will say things like 'I'm just SO angry', 'This is unbelievable' and 'I'm going to send an email.' The fuming stage often occurs at some sort of check-in desk and will result from hearing words such as 'overbooked' and 'no record of your reservation'. At this stage the Brit will be hot to the touch and quite clammy.

Stage 7: Seething

Very similar to fuming, but eerily quieter. Signs to look out for are teeth being ground to dust, watery eyes, and fists clenched so tightly they could turn coal into diamonds. Also listen out for slow, measured breathing through the nose. At this stage, if you prod the Brit, or suggest that perhaps they should just try to calm down a little bit, they will explode into stage 8 . . .

Stage 8: Bloody livid

'I AM CALM!' the Brit will now scream to the sky, before ripping off their jacket, screwing it into a ball and throwing it in the nearest fire. They might wrench the telly off the wall, or randomly start clearing full plates of hot food into the bin. They'll attempt to slam a door that is designed to always close gently, making them even more angry. They'll also go and sit in the car for no reason, before coming back inside again.

Stage 9: Going ballistic

The Brit will often misremember this stage, and will report back to family and friends, as the story gets retold every year for the rest of time, that they went 'absolutely ballistic'. What will have actually happened is they threw a bit of a hissy fit, refused to move and had to be taken to a side office to calm down as nearby children whispered, 'Daddy, why's that man stamping on his own phone?'

Stage 10: Silence

Leave the silent Brit well alone. He is a coiled adder. She is a firework that hasn't gone off. Do not approach. Leave in a dark room for three to four days and hope for the best.

8. SOCIAL MEDIA AND TECHNOLOGY

Only logging in to post what you had for lunch and accidentally ending up embroiled in a 12-hour debate about Jeremy Corbyn.

Accidentally liking someone's tweet and having to throw your phone in the bin.

Working on your computer while standing up for a few minutes, to ease everyone into the fact that you're about to leave for lunch.

9 p.m. Tired
10 p.m. Bed
11 p.m. Twitter
Midnight One more scan of Twitter
1 a.m. Switch to Facebook
2 a.m. Quick check of Instagram
4 a.m. Oh, no . . .

'I was listening!'
Translation: I could hear sounds coming
from you while I stared at my phone.

Whispering 'Oh, come on' to your computer, so everyone knows there's a problem that's out of your hands.

Adopting the manners of a *Downton Abbey* character when interacting with an elderly person on Facebook.

The tension of showing someone a series of photos on your phone and hoping you don't slide across one too many times.

'You look different to your profile
picture.'
'Yes, because that's from my prime
in 2007.'

Getting trapped in a WhatsApp group
chat until the day you die.

Only ever using the thumbs-up
'like' on Facebook because you
deem the other responses too
showy.

Sitting perfectly still in terrified silence until the unknown number stops ringing and goes away.

Putting something a bit zany in your bio and instantly feeling slightly disappointed in yourself.

Closing all your tabs with the panic of a dog protecting his bone when someone starts approaching your computer.

Posting 'Thanks for all the birthday wishes, y'all x!' and making a mental note not to say 'y'all' next year.

Trying to hold a casual conversation about why someone wants to borrow your iPad for the eight seconds it takes to delete all history.

Ending telephone conversations by saying 'Thanks' for no reason whatsoever.

Wondering with shame why you opted to post every picture you ever took for the entirety of 2007–2012.

'Give them a ring!'
'I've emailed.'
'Be quicker to ring.'
'I've sent a text as well.'
'Just ring them.'
'I'll send another email.'

Wondering why Richard Branson hasn't headhunted you despite your GCSE results being on clear view in your LinkedIn profile.

9. DIETING

Knowing it's time to diet when putting on a suit is like trying to dress a waterbed.

Deciding to rein in your ready meals from 'Family Size' to 'Serves 2'.

Trying to eat healthily in January when the cupboard still contains two tubs of chocolates, three tins of shortbread and half a pack of mince pies.

Waiting until everyone's gone to bed before leaning into the fridge and eating a block of Cheddar as if it's an apple.

Watching helplessly as you accept a tiny bit more at someone's house and are spooned an entirely new meal.

Opening a new packet of biscuits and being unable to help gathering the broken fragments of the top three and tidying them into your face.

Being so shocked at how many calories are in wine that you give up food immediately.

Preparing for a diet by emptying the entire contents of the fridge into your mouth.

Entering your daily calorie intake into a fitness app but missing off all the crisps in case it gets cross with you.

Moving your smart scales from the tiled floor to the bath mat to quickly lose several stone.

Deciding to go on a juice diet and drinking nothing but Um Bongo until friends force you to stop.

Saying 'I tend to put weight on my bum and my tummy', as opposed to your ears, knees and feet.

Entering into denial, anger, bargaining, depression and, after a long time, acceptance at just how many calories are in every type of cheese.

Modifying the 5:2 diet to 7:0 to better suit your lifestyle.

Ramping up your healthy eating to the point of throwing away two avocados a day.

Deciding to ruin every meal by sprinkling a handful of sunflower seeds over it.

Reading about the immense
health benefits of sweet potato, so
immediately making one into chips
and deep-frying them.

**Completely cutting bread from
your diet, with the exception
of toast, garlic baguettes and
sandwiches.**

The sad realisation that 'super' in 'super foods' is not a synonym for 'tasty'.

Using this little song to help remember which foods are mainly carbs: 'It's all the stuff that you like to eat.'

10. PETS

Going into a pet shop for a bag of food and coming out with an ultra-tough travel bed, a glow-in-the-dark lead, a sack of dried pig's ears, a fish tank and a rabbit.

Being required by law to engage in the 'He/she's lovely! What breed? How old?' canine chat routine at every opportunity.

Trying to politely end a conversation while your dog sprints off towards the horizon.

'Come on then, let's get you home.' Translation: Let's use you as an excuse to leave this boring stranger.

Feeling obliged to say 'Oh, he's all right' as your friend's dog chews through your arm.

Feeling a mixture of relief and hurt when you've braced yourself for dog talk and the other owner just walks straight past you.

'I can't believe how sharp its claws are.'
Translation: Your cat is making my arm resemble mince.

Wondering how your cat can bring half an hour of belly rubbing to a close by looking at you as if you're a prat and storming off.

Realising you haven't heard any dog noises for at least a minute, meaning that whichever room it's in will by now be completely destroyed.

'Airing cupboard.'
Translation: Cat sauna.

Knowing the question 'What's he rolling in?' is never going to result in a pleasant answer.

Vet: 'Well, your pet seems perfectly happy to me! That'll be £86, please.'

Being very theatrical about whipping out a poo bag, so everyone you suspect is secretly observing knows you're extremely responsible.

Thinking you're some kind of animal whisperer because you managed to stroke someone's pet without it mauling you.

Cat hasn't been seen for three days: 'I'm sure she's fine.'
Dog hasn't been seen for three seconds: 'Hello, police?'

Being unable to think of a more terrifying question to be asked than 'Has anyone seen my snake?'

Wondering why people go to the effort of picking up poo in a bag, tying up the bag and then depositing the bag on the floor.

Watching as your dog releases some pent-up energy by running at full speed in a straight line until he disappears completely.

'Please can we have a puppy?!'
Translation: Please can you buy, care for
and clean up after a puppy that I'll stroke
when convenient.

Wondering why your dog
translates 'Come!' as 'Run as fast
as you can to the other side of
the park and ruin that family's
picnic ... Quick, there's no time to
lose!'

11. THE VERY BRITISH 'HOW TO' GUIDE TO EVERYTHING

All you need to know to master any Very British situation

How to eat biscuits

1. Open packet
2. Tidy broken ones into mouth
3. Have one more
4. Have another
5. Finish all biscuits
6. Open new biscuits

How to answer the door

1. See person has arrived
2. Wait for doorbell
3. Count to five
4. Open and act surprised

How to fix a computer

1. Whisper 'Oh, come on'
2. Stand, lean over it and glare at the back
3. Click mouse six times/thrash it around a bit
4. Call IT

How to ruin a Brit's lunch break

'Just popping out for lunch.'
'I'll come with you.'

How to fix something

1. Say 'Let's have a look'
2. Describe the brokenness
3. Break it a bit more
4. Say 'Nah, it's broken'
5. Place hands on hips

Procedure for staring out of a window

1. Fold arms
2. Look at sky
3. Frown
4. Tut
5. Shake head
6. Say 'I don't know'
7. Walk away

How to avoid an old friend in the street

1. Commit to looking dead ahead
2. Hold imaginary conversation with yourself in your head
3. Check watch/phone as you pass
4. You're safe now

How to make the perfect cup of tea

Do it yourself

Ways to say 'I won't be coming'

1. I might pop down
2. I'll give you a text
3. I'll see how I feel
4. Sounds interesting

Procedure for being unthanked for door holding

1. Keep eyes fixed on culprit
2. Say 'You're welcome'
3. Shake head
4. Mutter 'Unbelievable'

How to exit the wrong shop

1. Walk around for five minutes
2. Check a price tag
3. Furrow brow and say 'Hmm'
4. Check watch
5. Thank nobody in particular
6. Leave

How to deal with a heatwave

1. Unbutton jacket
2. Look pained
3. Moan about it
4. Occasionally look at sky and shake head
5. Remember it'll rain again soon

How to make a Brit stay in a supermarket for hours

Ask them to get you a sandwich and say you don't mind which

How to wave back to someone

1. Raise and wave your hand
2. Realise they weren't waving at you
3. Leave country immediately

Dealing with strong wind

1. Frown at it
2. Order people to listen to it
3. Hunch shoulders
4. Turn slightly sideways
5. Sacrifice umbrella to it

How to make changing bed sheets enjoyable

It's impossible

Procedure when freshly seated on train

1. Exhale to show that you hurried
2. Wipe imaginary crumbs off thigh
3. Check watch
4. Fold arms
5. Close eyes
6. You're safe now

How to make it rain

1. Look at washing line
2. Clean car
3. Decide against umbrella
4. Nip out for lunch
5. Plan barbecue

How to exit a window seat

1. Lean forward
2. Gently touch headrest or bag
3. Whisper 'Sorry'
4. If procedure fails, stay on train for ever

How to answer a phone

1. Wait for it to stop ringing
2. Text 'Sorry, did you just call?'

How to deal with hay fever

1. Rub eyes until purple
2. Apologise for swollen face
3. Say 'Bloody hay fever' a lot

12. EATING OUTSIDE

Smelling sausages cooking in another postcode and immediately driving in a straight line to the supermarket's meat aisle.

Noting that the condiments on display at your friend's barbecue all seem to be labelled 'Best Before 1998'.

Knowing that eating two burgers, three hot dogs and five drumsticks inside would be ridiculously gluttonous, but that luckily calories don't count outside.

Trying to deal with a wasp when you have a glass in one hand and a plate in the other by sinking into a limbo position and screaming.

'I think this chicken might be a bit undercooked.'
Translation: I took one bite then emailed work to say I won't be in for a while.

Helping someone with the
barbecue by standing at their side
with your hands on your hips.

Not feeling very Continental at
all as a table umbrella sails across
the lawn and smashes through the
shed window.

Spending twice as much time cling-filming everything than you did actually eating.

Regretting the decision to eat outside when you lose all feeling in your hands.

Hoping your hosts are unaware that the packet of sausages you're taking over retail for 19p.

Regretting saying yes to 'Are you sure you're all right facing the sun?' when you finish your pub lunch with a head resembling an unopened Babybel.

'We thought we might have a barbecue for the Wimbledon final, if you fancy?'
'No thanks, I'll be watching tennis.'

Making 5 kg of couscous then throwing away 4.98 kg of couscous.

Thinking you may have walked too far while trying to find the perfect picnic spot when you see signs for the ferry.

'I think these burgers might be done.'
Translation: I just prodded one and nearly broke my finger.

Attempting to gallantly remove a fly from someone's Pimm's and ending up elbow deep in fruit.

Trying to re-create your holiday on the Med by dipping your bread in a pot of Hellman's.

Cutting short every meal outside to desperate shouts of 'GET THE CUSHIONS IN!'

Thinking a seagull understands what 'go away' means.

Wondering why you imagined a packet of six buns would suffice for 48 sausages.

13. MOVING HOUSE

Being loath to get rid of any clothes despite the chances of you fitting in them again being dependent on time travel.

Wondering why you decided that 'house stuff' would be a helpful thing to label 17 boxes.

Taking a box from the attic in your old house to the attic in your new house.

Spending four hours online choosing a toaster to go in the flat you chose after four minutes of viewing.

Questioning your packing ability
when you notice that one huge box
only contains half a bottle of ketchup,
a Rubik's cube and a handful of old
birthday cards.

**Finding it quite uncomfortable
when you, your partner and
the estate agent are all in the
bathroom taking it in turns to say
'Excellent'.**

Having to take responsibility and
apologise to the movers for the
laws of physics.

Wondering if anyone will ever invent
a box suitable for transporting the big
pepper grinder.

Thinking it was a mistake to help
carry the washing machine when
you spend the rest of the month
walking like you're still carrying
the washing machine.

Never feeling more like Tim Peake
than when you shrink your duvets
in a vacuum bag.

**Transporting the kettle in the
front seat of the car with you like
it's some kind of god.**

Filling a carrier bag with cables dating
back to 1978.

Demonstrating to the estate agent that you know exactly what you're doing by tapping firmly on any wall you encounter.

Finding out that 'great transport links' means 'your driveway is a bus stop'.

Discovering on the first night that your new home isn't in range of a single well-established pizza delivery service, so choosing between 'Monsieur Pizza', 'Ace Pizz-A!' and 'Toppy's'.

Simply accepting it when the estate agent says 'No, but you could easily install one' about every single thing you ask.

Making sure the movers know you're keen to help by carrying pillows, a sheet of paper and the cheese grater down to the van.

Wondering what state of mind you were in when you individually wrapped 24 shot glasses in newspaper.

Using a room to temporarily store half-emptied boxes until you decide to move house again.

Knowing the moving process is only truly over when you thoroughly resent every single thing you own.

14. FESTIVALS

The most unfulfilled plan of all time: 'Let's just take it easy on the first night.'

Wondering why the teenage boy is trying to direct you into a parking space as if he's marshalling an Airbus A380.

Feeling your heart sink when the band says 'Okay, we're going to play some new songs now.'

Picking a camping plot with a
steeper gradient than Everest.

Realising you've spent a fortune to stand around for the weekend in various queues.

Finding yourself paying £7 for a pitta bread full of grated carrot and hummus.

Opening each toilet door as if it's the door to a ferociously burning building.

Never having a more severe existential crisis than when cleaning your teeth outside your tent at 6 a.m. on day two.

**Considering three bags of
Frazzles and a can of warm cider
to be a sensible breakfast choice.**

Feeling like your life is at rock bottom
when you're desperately pumping blue
water over your own poo as though trying
to launch a boat with a watering can.

Assuring everyone that 'It's meant
to clear up a bit this afternoon' as
you watch your food, belongings
and spouse drift off to sea.

'Okay, shall we meet by this pole at 1?'
Translation: I guess this is goodbye for ever.

Paying £180 to sit cross-legged on the ground picking and throwing bits of grass for three days.

Being unable to find your tent and panicking as if you've been abandoned on Mars.

Feeling extremely envious of people who can be bothered to shower when they arrive back at the tent full of joy.

Thinking nothing transforms you from 'office worker' to 'free-love bohemian' quite so powerfully as a floppy hat.

Discovering that your tent's been ransacked and used as a toilet, before remembering that's how you left it.

Really getting into the spirit of things by watching your favourite band with your arms folded while nodding your head slightly.

**Considering the highlight of
the festival to be when you sat
in the car for a bit with the air
conditioning on.**

Washing with wet wipes so you
now smell like a farm animal *and*
wet wipes.

Reviewing every single food stall as 'Not
great'.

15. THE BIZARRE BRITISH PUB NAME GAME

One pub is real, one is completely made up ... can you guess which are the actual drinking dens?

1. The Cock & Womble *or* The Cock & Bull
2. The Bum & Fluff *or* The Round Bush
3. The Roaring Donkey *or* The Screaming Lion

4. The Tale of the Thrusting Trousers *or* The Legend of Oily Johnnies
5. I Am the Only Running Footman *or* I Am the Only Dancing Huntsman
6. The Swan with Two Necks *or* The Duck with Two Beaks
7. The Dog & Jelly Mould Tavern *or* The Cat & Custard Pot Inn
8. The Crooked Billet *or* The Wonky Leg
9. The Pub with No Name *or* The Pub That's Not There
10. The Long Road to Bethlehem *or* Ye Olde Trip to Jerusalem
11. Poosie Nansie's *or* Weesie Grannie's
12. The Archaeologist's Legs *or* The Pyrotechnist's Arms

13. The Hippo & the Plumber *or* The Walrus & the Carpenter

14. The Duke of Coward City *or* The Mayor of Scaredy Cat Town
15. Bob's Yer Uncle *or* Gordon Bennett!
16. The Camels Purse *or* The Otters Pocket

The actual real pubs are . . .

1. The Cock & Bull (Sutton)
2. The Round Bush (Watford)
3. The Roaring Donkey (Clacton-on-Sea)
4. The Legend of Oily Johnnies (Workington)
5. I Am the Only Running Footman (London)
6. The Swan with Two Necks (Blackbrook, Staffordshire)
7. The Cat & Custard Pot Inn (Tetbury)
8. The Crooked Billet (Milton Keynes)
9. The Pub with No Name (Petersfield)
10. Ye Olde Trip to Jerusalem (Nottingham)
11. Poosie Nansie's (Mauchline)
12. The Pyrotechnist's Arms (London)
13. The Walrus & the Carpenter (London)
14. The Mayor of Scaredy Cat Town (London)
15. Gordon Bennett! (Surbiton)
16. The Otters Pocket (Stamford)

16. SICKNESS AND HEALTH

Doctor: 'How's your diet?'

You: 'Fine, quite varied.'

Translation: Crisps, sweets, cheese, tea, booze, pies and sometimes an apple.

Hoping that when you're advised to follow a Mediterranean diet, it mainly involves drinking ouzo on a sunlounger until you fall asleep.

Signalling to the dentist that you're feeling excruciating, white-hot, intense, all-consuming pain by closing one eye slightly.

'I feel a bit rough actually.'
Translation: I think I might be dead.

Being told that tea and wine can
badly stain your teeth so making a
mental note to buy some straws.

Being in a perpetual state of thinking you
have a cold coming on.

'We have an appointment
available at 10 a.m.'
'Is that with a doctor?'
'No, it's with . . .'
'Because I saw a medical student
last time.'
'This will be with one of the
cleaners.'

The pharmacy: a room full of
people all facing in completely
different directions, so everyone
knows they're not in the queue.

Automatically saying 'How are you
feeling?' to the person lying in a full body
cast in the hospital bed.

Making up for half a decade
of slapdash dental hygiene by
brushing your teeth for four
hours before your appointment.

Never feeling more ashamed than
when handing a receptionist a jar
of your own warm urine.

'Does it hurt when I press here?'
'No, I love having thumbs
pressed into my face.'

Being told not to eat before a blood
test so strictly only having one
Weetabix.

'I've never been in this much pain before.'
'Maybe you should go to hospital?'
'I'll be fine.'

Doctor: 'How often do you exercise?'

You: 'I used to be in the school rugby team!'

Doctor: 'Sir, you're forty-three.'

'Ever experience trouble passing a stool?'
'Only if it's heavy and there are pint glasses all over the table.'

Going to a physiotherapy appointment that seems to 100 per cent involve bending the knee that it hurts to bend.

Literally putting your spine in the hands of someone who appears to have a chiropractic certificate from Backs R Us.

Meeting someone who's a GP and immediately showing them the strange mole on your bum, despite being in a café.

Feeling extremely smug after being the best at pulling over to let an ambulance pass.

17. MEETINGS

Wondering if your boss is really invested in you when he combines your yearly appraisal with a trip to the vending machine.

Having a meeting to discuss what happened in the last meeting and what to prepare for the next meeting.

Deciding to unfold your arms in a meeting, in case you're coming across as too aggressive.

Arriving late to find no free seats then instantly regretting your painful decision to crouch.

Saying 'Sounds good to me' then
quickly realising a lot more was
expected from you.

'I'll make a note of it.'
Translation: Let's never speak of it again.

'Company meeting.'
Translation: By the end of today
you'll either be fired or have to
move house.

The horror: 'Right, do you want to start us
off?'

Knowing it's not a proper meeting until you've underlined the word 'meeting' at least eight times.

Suddenly being asked for your thoughts when you've spent the last 15 minutes thinking about which sandwich to have for lunch.

'Let's leave that for now.'
Translation: Please stop talking.

The heartbreak when you have a lunch meeting and the most important person orders water.

The giddy, childlike euphoria when someone brings biscuits into a meeting room.

Having that one colleague who requests
you send them a calendar invite for the
quick chat you've asked for in five minutes'
time.

'Tentative.'
Translation: I'm yet to think of an
excuse.

**Wondering how many more
hours into the conference call you
should leave it before revealing
you haven't heard a single word.**

'I'm afraid he's in a meeting at the minute, can I take a message?'
Translation: He's at his desk gesturing wildly at me.

'Can I just borrow you?'
Translation: You're not in trouble.
'Can I just grab you?'
Translation: You might be in trouble.
'Can I have a quick word?'
Translation: You're fired.

Knowing a meeting isn't officially over until someone senior has said 'Thanks, guys.'

The peculiar ending
of all meetings:
'Okay, everyone
happy?'
(Complete silence.)
'Excellent!'

18. EMAIL TRANSLATION GUIDE

A handy jargon-buster for your inbox . . .

Subject lines

'FYI'
Nothing to do with me

     'Quick reminder'
     I don't trust you to know what's going on

'Do you have two minutes?'
I have unsettling news, and I'll actually
need half an hour

'Working from home'
I'm lying on the sofa watching *Loose Women*

'Leaving card'
Any second now you'll be asked to give £5 to someone you don't know

'Last night ...'
... Was a mistake

'Your order will be delivered today'
You will miss your delivery today

'Next week . . .'
I'm going on holiday and I'm about to give
you all my work

'I'm running a 5K!'
I expect you to pay for my new hobby

'Where is everyone?'
I've come in on a bank holiday, haven't I?

'Pub?'
Let's go drink and complain about our
colleagues

Introductions

'Dear Sirs'
I don't think any women work in your
office because I'm from the eighteenth
century

'Hi there'
I couldn't be bothered to look up your
name

'Greetings!'
I'm zany!

'I hope this email finds you well'
I want to go straight into what this email
is about but I don't have the confidence

'I'm good, thanks, hope you are too'
Let's get to the point now

'Thanks for your email'
I got your email and unfortunately I'm not
in a position to ignore it

'Morning!!!'
I've had a lot of coffee

'Dear valued good friend'
I'm about to offer you the chance to send
me money on the promise of $57m

> 'I was just wondering if you happened to
> know by any chance if . . .'
> I love typing

General e-speak

'Did you get a chance to see my last
email?'
Please stop ignoring me

> 'With all due respect'
> You're talking absolute codswallop

'As no doubt you're aware'
Everybody knows about the bad thing
I/you/the company have done

'Is anyone able to tell me why . . .'
Someone's going to get it in the neck

'Sorry, would help if I actually attached it
this time!'
I have never managed to properly attach a
file to an email

'Everything should be in my handover'
Contact me at your peril

'With very limited access to email'
Seriously, go away

Sign-offs

'Look forward to hearing your thoughts'
I'm hoping your only thought is 'Yes,
that's fine'

'I'll leave it with you'
I'm washing my hands of all responsibility

'All my best'
I like you

'All best'
I like you but I want you to see I'm busy

'Best'
I hate you

'Warmest regards'
I'm a bit odd

'Kind regards'
I'm on autopilot

'Regards'
I've had just about enough of your shit

'Many thanks'
Actually just one thanks

'Cheers'
I'm enormously chilled out about the
whole situation

'Thanks'
Just do it

'Thanks in advance!'
Do it yesterday

19. BUYING A CAR

'What sort of thing are you looking for?'
'Well, just . . . I mean . . . I suppose . . . maybe . . . a car?'

'What will you be using it for?'
'Driving about, mostly.'

Being more nervous during a test drive than you were on your actual driving test.

Being extremely embarrassed as soon as
the words 'Ooh, it smells nice' leave your
lips.

**Feeling the need to do a little
pretend drive even though you're
sitting in a stationary car on a
forecourt.**

'Can you go lower on the price?'

'No, I'm afraid not.'

'Okay, I think we have ourselves a deal.'

Anxiously waiting for your dad to tell you all the reasons why you've bought a mistake.

Feeling too awkward to ask the hardball questions the money-saving website suggested, so just saying 'Will it come with some petrol?'

Feeling like the king of haggling when the dealer says they'll even throw in the handbook and the keys for free.

Wondering how many of his pals the car salesman has told about you.

Asking how many miles to the gallon the car does, despite not knowing how many miles to the gallon any of your previous cars did. Or what a gallon is.

Noting that the car you want is in Road Tax Band E, meaning ... something, surely?

Wondering what the salesman's thinking as you inspect a tyre by squeezing it with your hand.

Buying an all-terrain four-wheel drive mountain-rescue vehicle for your weekly trip to Tesco.

Feeling like an idiot as everyone watches you test out the back seats by having a sit in them for 10 seconds.

Feeling the need to literally shake on it, despite the 100 pieces of paper you still have to sign.

Buying a base level of car insurance that covers everything except windscreen, wing mirrors, wheels, engine, chassis, seats, exhaust and electrics.

Wondering how every single vehicle you look at seems to have been awarded Car of the Year.

Finding your new car's controls so unfamiliar that you spend the first month thanking other drivers by spraying water all over your windscreen.

Choosing your new car based purely on whether or not the dog will like it.

20. WATCHING SPORT

Insisting on digging out the
replica kit you bought for Euro 96,
despite it fitting more snugly than
Sellotape.

Spending the entirety of a rugby match shouting 'Surely that's a knock-on?' because you don't really understand what's happening.

Thinking that if you really stress the three syllables in 'REF-ER-EE!' you'll sound like the world's greatest football pundit.

Instantly regretting your decision to lie and say you watched the game after you're asked for your detailed analysis of the second goal.

Deciding this will be the year you finally go to watch Wimbledon, purely for the opportunity of standing in the world's most prestigious queue.

Watching the start of the F1 and then wishing the rest of the race was as exciting.

Deciding to watch the Super Bowl and understanding about as much of what's going on as a dog watching a roller coaster.

Folding your arms and remaining silent for at least five minutes after Hawk-Eye corrects your vehement declaration that 'That was miles out!'

Finally biting the bullet and buying the sports channels, a day before a new, even more expensive sports channel decides to buy all the sports.

Deciding to have a punt on the Grand National because you have a good feeling about ... Oh, he's fallen at the first fence again.

Watching the finest Olympic athletes in the world while lying down with a plate of biscuits balanced on your belly.

Saying 'I could have scored that!' when the last time you tried to kick a ball you dislocated your leg without making any connection.

Coming a cropper when you're asked what league the team you claim to support are in these days and reply with 'I'm not sure, you know.'

Feeling like you've blown your
cover as a fair-weather gambler
when you go into the bookie's
and ask 'Is it okay if I place a bet?'

Knowing you can make your team
score simply by leaving the room
for three seconds.

Being unable to watch cricket
without occasionally lunging
around the room miming forward
defensive shots with your arm.

Being unable to help saying 'London Marathon this weekend' to everyone you know, despite having no interest in running at all.

Offering your expert commentary of 'He's so quick!' while watching Usain Bolt run the 100 metres in record time.

Claiming you're watching the golf when really you just wanted to have a nice sit-down for six hours.

Pressing the red button during a tennis match, causing your television to freeze for an hour and a half.

21. TEA TIMELINE

Join us on a journey through the world's greatest ever liquid

1662

Welcome, tea! It's all go for tea in the seventeenth century. Catherine Braganza of Portugal marries Charles II; she loves a good cuppa and introduces it to the English court. Just as it is today, tea is considered a cure-all for many conditions. Hurray for tea!

1700s

Tea begins to replace ale as the drink of choice at breakfast. Boo to tea.

1717

Thomas Twining (that surname rings a bell) opens the Golden Lyon in London, the first tea shop in England. However, it's still only a drink for the rich, with 100 g of Twinings Gunpowder Green Tea going for £160, which means a single Hobnob probably cost about £3,000.

1840

By the nineteenth century, people were starting to feel a bit peckish between the two main meals of the day, breakfast and dinner. Step forward hungry genius Anna, 7th Duchess of Bedford, who said 'Hang on, I'll have a cup of tea and a sandwich in my room while nobody's watching.' Just like that, afternoon tea was born.

1890s

How to pimp tea? Add a shot of rum. This is exactly what British Army soldiers did during the 1890s before a morning attack and also to celebrate passing-out parades.

1904

The 1904 World's Fair in St Louis was hot. Proper hot. This led to Richard Blechynden, a merchant and tea plantation owner, serving a cool version of tea that sold like hot cakes (or cold cakes) and gained national popularity. In the USA today, iced tea makes up 85% of all tea swallowed. In the UK it's not even nearly as widely consumed, for the reason that it's not proper tea and never will be, so there.

Also in 1904, vacuum flasks were first manufactured for commercial use when two German glassblowers formed Thermos, meaning Brits everywhere could begin the habit of buying one, taking it to work and then forgetting to take it out of their drawer for ever.

1908

The tea bag was first successfully
marketed by tea and coffee importer
Thomas Sullivan from New York, with
the tea contained in bags of silk. It took
until 1944 for tea bags to be rectangular
and no longer resembling small sacks.

1914–1918

During the First World War, the diet of
British soldiers consisted of rations such
as cheese, jam, sugar, salt, condensed milk
and, most importantly, tea, which was
vital as it concealed the taste of water that
was often transported in petrol cans.

1946

George Orwell publishes his essay 'A Nice Cup of Tea' in the *Evening Standard*. It lists 11 rules for making the perfect cuppa. Pros: he's a milk-in-last man; cons: at no point does he mention the necessity of chocolate digestives. 5/10.

1953

Tea bags are sold in Britain, thanks to Tetley. After 36 years of drinking tea, vigorous scratching of foreheads, complex calculation and trips back to the drawing board, the company launches the round tea bag in 1989.

1955

This year saw the launch of arguably the most ground-breaking and important invention of all time, the first fully automatic kettle, the K1 from Russell Hobbs. Before the K1, heating water with electricity was potentially quite dangerous. In 1960, the second most important invention ever was unveiled: the K2 (also a kettle).

1990

The largest ever UK TV pickup (a phenomenon whereby large numbers of people watching the same telly show use an ad break to operate electrical appliances: in Britain this means kettles) is recorded during the England v West Germany semi-final penalty shoot-out in the 1990 World Cup. Unfortunately no amount of tea could prevent inevitable disaster.

2010

The biggest cup of tea ever was made in Sri Lanka, containing 4,000 litres (or 7,039 pints) of the brown stuff. The cup itself was ten feet high and eight feet wide: a nightmare to wash. Any biscuits dropped in this tea required a four-day rescue mission. Britain's excuse for not making the largest cup of tea itself was reported to be 'I'm sure we made the last one.'

2013

The launch of the iKettle, the Wi-Fi-enabled water heater that you can control by app, lets tea fans boil water remotely from any room in their house using their phones. They can then forget they've done it and leave the house.

2015

British astronaut Tim Peake tweets from space: 'Found my tea . . . life is good!' When asked what it tastes like, he gives the emphatic review: 'OK.'

2016

Guinness World Records confirms the discovery in China of the world's oldest tea leaves. The leaves, which we imagine were a bit musty, were buried with Emperor Liu Qi and aged over 2,100 years. Also found in the tomb is a past-its-best Kit Kat, as well as a very crinkled copy of *Gardener's World*, which is moved straight to the nearest dentist's waiting room.

2024

Someone launches the octagonal tea bag. Consumers claim the tea companies have finally started to run out of ideas.

2035

First cup of tea is consumed on Mars, making the front page of all the newspapers in Britain. On page two of all the newspapers is the headline: 'Martians exist'.

2044

Everyone collectively admits that after much deliberation and heroic attempts to enjoy it, nobody actually likes green tea after all.

2052

Tea runs out and the world ends. Not ideal.

22. SHOPPING

Walking from car park to shop repeatedly
saying 'Could've parked there, look.'

'Look, it didn't come with a
returns label!'
Translation: I threw it in the bin.

Wondering why clothes shops feel
the need to keep the fitting room
temperatures set to 'Sahara'.

Wondering if the delivery man knows the
box he's handing you contains 180 toilet
rolls.

The unwritten understanding that you'll only go to your nearest shopping centre if there's a McFlurry involved somewhere.

Hoping that briskly walking three steps across the shop floor will prove an adequate test for the six years you'll have your new shoes.

Going to a garden centre purely
to have a fry-up and to look at the
hot tubs again.

**Wondering how IKEA keep
getting away with making
customers work in its warehouse.**

'All these tops are a funny shape.'
Translation: I'm a funny shape.

Being required by law to ask 'Was town busy?' to anyone recently returned from town.

Knowing you're getting older when your kind of clothes start to take up a smaller and smaller part of the shop.

Going into Sports Direct for a pair of
running socks and coming out with
an American football, a pair of boxing
gloves, an FC Barcelona shirt, a £3 cricket
bat and another giant mug.

Always making sure to specify
that you're going to 'big' Tesco.

Only ever describing
a trip into town one
of two ways:
1. 'It was dead.'
2. 'It was absolute
chaos.'

Buying a jacket a tiny bit too small
in the hope that your skeleton will
somehow reduce in size.

**Trying out a new mattress by
sitting on the edge and bouncing
up and down – something you'll
never, ever do with any mattress
you actually own.**

Knowing the key-cutting shop could pick
a number out of a hat and you'd still pay
it.

Thinking if you stand with your hands on your hips for long enough the flat-pack cabinet will suddenly decide to fit in your car.

Wondering if anyone has ever needed a shoe fixing and a key cutting at the same time.

Going into a shop that has approximately four items of clothing on show and immediately knowing it's out of your price range.

Realising the hard way that the electronic capacity signs outside shopping centre car parks aren't actually connected to anything.

23. HITTING THE TOWN

Feeling a huge wave of relief when the bouncer says your choice of shoes means you're not allowed in.

'Let's paint the town red!'
Translation: Let's sit quietly in the corner of one pub for six hours.

Hoping if you keep saying 'It's in the top ten on TripAdvisor' it'll make up for accidentally booking a meal in a motorway service station.

'Have you got cheese and onion?'
'No, but we've got stilton and port, Moroccan chicken and thyme, sweet chilli and basil or sea salt and kidney.'

'I'm about five minutes away.' Translation: I'm still in my bathroom.

Leaving restaurant: 'That was lovely.'
Outside: 'Well, it was okay.'
In car: 'I mean, it wasn't great.'
Back home: 'We won't go there again.'

'You can't book online, says you have to ring.'
'Shall we just stay in?'

Making the mistake of thinking a bar with multiple levels might be good.

Worrying that the comedian will catch your eye at a stand-up gig despite being in row 57.

Not having a clue what's going on while watching a Shakespeare play, despite Wiki-ing the plot beforehand.

Being teetotal on a boozy night out and
ingesting so many caffeinated drinks that
you start to see into the future.

Realising that the best part of
going out is drinking in front of
your bedroom mirror.

Clubbing: paying £15 to spend the night lowering your head and shouting 'Pardon?'

Going to a house party for the opportunity of drinking while standing in the corner of a stranger's kitchen.

Feeling your heart sink when you're informed of the imminent arrival of 'a bit of a character' who's 'fine once you get to know them'.

Thinking of alerting Trading Standards when the club's toilet hasn't got a lock, a lid, a door, a flush or even water.

Managing to eat a kebab
while swaying like a stationary
computer game character.

'What are you doing for New
Year?'
'Sitting quietly in my pyjamas.'

Never feeling less proud of yourself than when eating a Big Mac off a plate in the dark at 2 a.m.

Levels of hangover:
'Bit tired.'
'Bit rough, actually.'
'I've felt better, to be honest.'
'I can't see.'
'Never again.'
'Kill me.'
Silence.

24. BRITISH COCKTAIL RECIPES

The latest Very British liquid delights to add to your repertoire*

The Livener

You will need: four parts gin, one part vodka, straw
Method: pour all measures into nearby vessel (large glass, measuring jug, saucepan, whatever's handy), shake about a bit, hold nose and suck through straw until you feel worryingly warm. Not for the faint of leg. A cad's delight!
Ideal for: pre-dinner party
Hangover scale: 7–8

---

* Please do not try any of these drinks.

The Cheeky Commuter

You will need: coffee, dark rum, sugar cubes (8), half a Twix, Thermos flask

Method: prepare the night before by putting all ingredients and apparatus (including kettle) under your bed. Upon waking, place everything except the Twix in Thermos, add boiling water, attach lid and shake. Open on train; use Twix for dippin'. All aboard!

Ideal for: frosty winter Monday morns

Hangover scale: 3–4

Yellow Peril

You will need: advocaat, two bananas, English mustard, milk, ice, nearby unoccupied bathroom

Method: whack all the stuff in a blender and mix for as long as it takes to recite alphabet. To pass the time as ingredients pulverise, talk to a pretend camera in the style of your favourite celeb chef. Decant mixture into half an Easter egg and sip malevolently. Night fever!

Ideal for: crazy nights and lazy days

Hangover scale: unknown

Wine Surprise

You will need: any open bottle of red or white wine, a supermarket juice, salt
Method: fill half a pint glass with any nearby open wine you can find, then top up with fruit juice (orange squash works well). Once finished, lick salt off the worktop to remind you how low you've sunk. A perfect glugging drink!
Ideal for: standing over the sink
Hangover scale: 5–6

The 'Well This is Fun'

You will need: a plain glass, ice and lemon if you can be bothered, endless Diet Coke, sense of sadness
Method: pour Coke in glass and drink about 15 litres over a three-hour period. Drive everyone home and insist you had a nice time. A rank outsider!
Ideal for: January
Hangover scale: 0

The Sad Lady

You will need: gin, a cup (optional)
Method: sip gin by an open window.
Remember better times gone by. Remorse!
Ideal for: no one
Hangover scale: for ever

The Spicy Cuckoo

You will need: tomato juice, tequila, hot sauce, dry-roasted peanuts, garlic, pickle juice, absorbent paper towel
Method: place all ingredients in a blender and whizz for 30 seconds. Remove blender lid (warning: do not smell drink), pour straight into mouth. A real pick-me-up. Knock knock!
Ideal for: idiots and dreamers
Hangover scale: 9–10

Unfinished Business

You will need: bourbon, sherry, cherry Coke, juice of one lime, blackberries
Method: thrash the blackberries and lime in the bottom of a crystal tumbler, then add the booze and cola to taste. Drink while wearing a suit and speaking in a mid-American drawl. The height of transatlantic sophistication. Sell sell sell!
Ideal for: reading the papers
Hangover scale: 3–4

The Very British hangover scale

0: fresher than a daisy just washed in Lenor, sparkling

1–2: a mild tugging of the brain, a cheeky ghost in the cogs

3–4: a crow pecking in your ear, an invisible cloak of grease, mild sadness

5–6: spicy talons prod the hypothalamus, regret stains your jeans, eternal Tuesday

7–8: a real retching bastard in the glove box, 'Oh, God' mutterings, much wailing

9–10: a swift cricket bat to the temple, a gut punch of bile, pleading and bargaining, never again

25. JOB INTERVIEWS

Saying 'Hi, I'm here for the job interview?' so quietly and discreetly that it sounds like you're asking the receptionist for drugs.

Knowing you've blown it the second you panic and tell the interviewer to take a seat.

'Can I get you anything? Tea, coffee, water?'
'Lovely, thanks.'

Being too embarrassed to even practise
the 'Tell us a bit about yourself' question
at home, let alone answer it in the
interview.

'What are your weaknesses?'
'I don't like talking to people, I'm
silent in meetings and I'm rubbish
at doing stuff.'

**Instantly regretting your decision
to reply to 'It says on your CV
that you're proficient in computer
software' with 'Does it?!'**

Hobbies on CV: 'Running, reading and cooking.'
Actual hobbies: 'Staring at phone, eating and scratching myself.'

'I'm highly organised.'
Translation: I make sure to put everything into one big folder labelled 'work stuff'.

Concentrating so hard on maintaining determined-yet-not-scary eye contact that you completely miss all the questions.

Applying the advice that it's okay to take time to think before answering a bit too rigorously and ending up sitting in silence for a good five minutes.

Hoping your stripy socks will make up for your almost complete lack of personality.

'Why are you leaving your old job?'
'They wanted me to start doing some actual work.'

Revealing your ignorance surrounding internet culture when you pronounce 'meme' to rhyme with 'semi'.

Wondering if arguing with strangers on Twitter until you fall asleep counts as 'extensive knowledge of social media'.

Saying 'That's a very good question' and then staring at the ceiling for an unfortunate amount of time.

Knowing that 'Do you monitor internet usage?' sounds bad as soon as it leaves your lips.

'How do you deal with conflict?'
'I hide in the toilet until it's blown over.'

'What are your strengths?'
'I put a lot of effort into looking like I
know what I'm doing.'

Internally debating whether it
would be awfully rude to enquire
about how much you might
hypothetically be paid.

**Looking at your notes when you
leave and realising you forgot to
mention everything.**

26. SUNDAYS

Getting into a four-hour argument over what does and does not belong in a Full English.

Knowing before you even open
your eyes that you forgot to buy
bacon.

Spending the day relaxing to the soothing
sound of a football thudding against your
fence.

**Wishing the weather would turn
colder to give your roast dinner
maximum impact.**

Waking up to what appears to be someone from your street having a bonfire somewhere in your bedroom.

Agreeing to go for a Sunday walk before discovering there's no pub element.

Saturday: 'Looking forward to a
lie-in tomorrow!'
Sunday: Wide awake by 6 a.m.

Marvelling at just how fast your
neighbour's grass must grow to warrant
the nine hours he spends mowing it every
Sunday.

'I'll see how I feel.'
Translation: I won't be there.

Suddenly panicking that you haven't done your homework on Sunday evenings, despite being 36.

Suspecting you may have roasted the vegetables for too long when a gentle fork prod causes them to shatter into dust.

Thinking 'But I've got all the papers to get through' is a valid excuse for getting out of any commitment.

Saying 'I hope you don't mind it well done' as you notice your beef joint is now the size and texture of a tennis ball.

'What time does the supermarket close?'
'4 p.m.'
'I thought it was 5?!'

Greeting your neighbour with a cheery 'Oh, hello!' after spending Saturday night violently banging on their wall.

Finding yourself saying 'Let's go for a drive!' despite commuting by car for 20 hours a week.

Never being more apologetic than when daring to ask for more gravy during pub lunch.

Suddenly realising you're in B&Q looking at various types of screws you don't even need.

Being spotted taking delivery of a gigantic pizza in your pyjamas and eating every slice with tremendous shame.

Hearing the *Antiques Roadshow* theme music and knowing the weekend is well and truly utterly dead.

27. CHRISTMAS

Complaining that Christmas starts too early while filling two trolleys with mince pies.

'Did you manage to have a think about what you'd like for Christmas yet?'
Translation: You're three minutes away from getting socks again.

Responding to 'Not long now!' by simply saying 'Don't'.

The extra-special treat of being allowed to go to work in a novelty jumper.

Wondering why 'Best Xmas Gifts!' guides assume you have about £400 to spend per present.

Spending most of December being ordered to get out of your own fridge.

Really getting into the festive spirit by draping an old bit of tinsel over your desk phone.

Most asked questions on 25 December:
1. 'Have we got any batteries?'
2. 'What is it?'
3. 'Can we watch something else?'

The crushing sense of doom
when someone asks you to
nip to the supermarket on
24 December.

Wondering what crime you committed
in a previous life to deserve having your
package delivered to a neighbour's house.

'How did the office Christmas
party go?'
'Yeah, I don't work there any more.'

The paralysing horror of encountering a weak flush while staying at someone else's house over the festive period.

Being unable to unwrap a bottle-shaped
present without first saying 'I think I
know what this is.'

Feeling compelled to describe
your gift as 'nothing' at the exact
moment you hand it over.

**Feeling the need to shout 'They're
here!' as the doorbell sounds
loudly around the house.**

Persuading everyone to play a board game and accidentally destroying your family.

Trying to remember the last time you ate something that wasn't on a cling-filmed plate in the fridge.

Christmas Eve diet: bits sneakily sliced and picked from the edges of things you're not allowed to eat yet.

Boxing Day breakfast: turkey, bit of ham, one pig in blanket, cold roast potato, what you assume is mash, cheese, half a parsnip, chocolate.

The great British back-to-work-after-Christmas catch-up chat:
'Good Christmas?'
'Yeah, quite quiet.'
(End.)

28. A–Z OF BRITAIN

A pocket guide to all the ingredients in the big British pie

Apologising

The national sport, practised all day every day, for ever. Sorry.

Boat race

An excuse to get sloshed while two canoes full of clever people thrash their way down the Thames.

Bog snorkelling

Whereby competitors swim two lengths of a watery trench cut through a peat bog as quickly as possible. Not to be confused with 'attending Glastonbury'.

Cheese rolling

A 9 lb Double Gloucester cheese travelling at up to 70 mph is chased down a hill.

Chips (eating of)

Not crisps. Not fries. Chips. Chip butties, fish and chips, cheesy chips, chips and gravy, chips and curry sauce. Wonderful chips.

Crufts

Where very tidy dogs join together to be stared at by humans, who eventually point at the one they like most.

Curling

Known as 'chess on ice' but really more 'bowls on ice, with sweeping'. Scots, the inventors of the sport, are the masters of it.

Donkey rides

The epitome of British seaside fun: a very slow ride on a little horse.

Eels

Best served by the sea in cold jelly. So delicious you'll rarely eat them, if ever.

Fry-ups

One of the most divisive meals in Britain. Brits will fall out for ever over optimum baked-bean ratio and inclusion of black/white pudding.

Guy Fawkes Night

Also known as Bonfire Night. Brits gather together in November to film fireworks displays on their phones, which they will never, ever watch again.

Hay fever

More commonly known as 'bloody hay fever', this ailment causes most Brits' faces to shut down for the summer months.

IKEA (endless visits to)

Also called the Meatball Place and Hotdog Heaven. Brits will spend their weekends here angrily buying sideboards that don't fit in the house.

Juniper berries

The key ingredient in gin, the cause of all problems.

Kettles (boiling of)

The solution to all problems.

Lifts

The most silent places in Britain.

Moaning (love of)

A Brit's most common form of exercise. Most will moan so often and vigorously that it burns an average of 2,000 calories a day.

Morris dancing

A very British version of karate.

Mowing

The art of spending a whole Saturday
mowing a rectangle of lawn no larger than
a table-tennis table.

Nettle eating

An actual stinging-nettle-eating contest
in Dorset. 2016's winner chomped 86 feet
of the painful salad, impressing some.

'Oh dear'

A Brit's response to the most devastating, life-ruining events and desperately unfortunate situations.

Pancake tossing

The skill of throwing solid discs of milk all over the kitchen worktop.

Picnics

The pursuit of walking for so long trying to find the perfect place to eat a pork pie that it gets dark and you have to go home again.

Pimm's

A Brit's way of getting their five-a-day during the week of summer.

Pub gardens

Or beer gardens. Often a square metre of concrete with a bench on it, filled with 100 people on warm days.

Queuing

The other national sport.

Rambling

Walking but with an extremely technical
waterproof jacket.

Roasts

Some slices of meat and some vegetables
on a plate, lauded as the peak of culinary
pleasure.

Straw Bear Festival

A man dressed in straw is led around town. Quite terrifying.

Street names (rude ones)

Minge Lane? Bell End? Crotch Crescent? Tee hee ...

Tar barrel carrying

The custom of carrying a flaming barrel of tar through the street, as the name wholly suggests.

Tea

Hot brown leaf liquid, aka the best thing in the world.

Umbrellas

Leave home without one and it'll chuck it down; leave home with one and you'll lose it. A sick game.

Vegetable growing

Nothing says 'page seven of the local paper' like an old man with a huge marrow.

Wasps (hatred of)

Nasty slim bees.

Wheelie bins (obsession with)

You're wondering if it's bin day right now, aren't you?

Wimbledon

Where sunburned folk gather together to shout 'Come on, Tim!' at a man named Andy.

Xylophones

Thinking of words beginning with x that aren't xylophone. Over to you.

Yolks

A split egg yolk or an underdone/overdone yolk will ruin a Brit's day. A double yolk will make their month.

Zebras

British ones.

ACKNOWLEDGEMENTS

In no particular order, firm handshakes and, if it's not too forward/awkward, pats on the back to the following: Everyone who follows Very British Problems (@SoVeryBritish) online; Adam Bunker; Juliet Mushens and Nathalie Hallam at Caskie Mushens; Andrew Wightman; Hannah Boursnell, Tamsyn Berryman and everyone at Little, Brown/Sphere. Now let's never mention this again.